MW01152608

ARE ALL BACTERIA DANGEROUS?

Biology Book for Kids
Children's Biology Books

BABY PROFESSOR

EDUCATION KIDS

Speedy Publishing LLC

40 E. Main St. #1156

Newark, DE 19711

www.speedypublishing.com

Copyright 2017

All Rights reserved. No part of this book may be reproduced or used in any way or form or by any means whether electronic or mechanical, this means that you cannot record or photocopy any material ideas or tips that are provided in this book.

In this book, we're going to cover information about different types of bacteria. So, let's get right to it!

BACTERIA ILLUSTRATION

WHAT ARE BACTERIA?

As you get dressed, eat breakfast and go to school, all around you there is a hidden world. Bacteria are microorganisms that can only be seen through a microscope. It's a good thing for us that this is the case because if not, we would see millions of them all around us.

They're floating in the air, they're traveling on our skin, they're on the ground, they're in our food and water, and they live in every plant and animal on Earth. In fact, there are ten times more bacterial cells than human cells in your body!

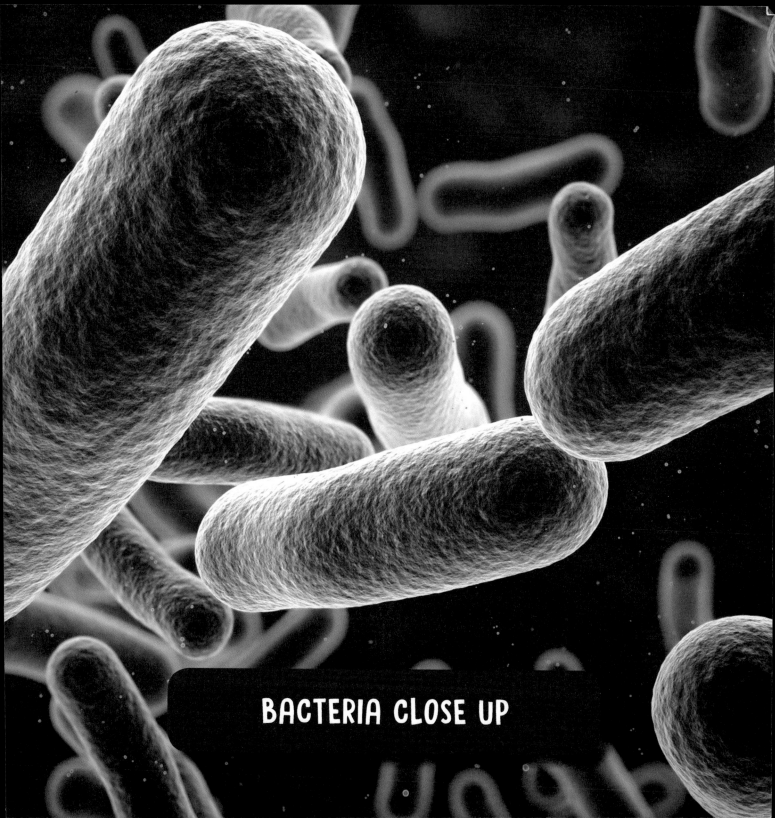

BACTERIA CLOSE UP

BACTERIA

Bacteria are very simple prokaryotic microorganisms. Prokaryotic simply means that their cell structure is very basic. Their cells don't have a nucleus "command center" that tells the cell what to do. Unlike the cells of plants and animals, their cells don't have lots of organelles that take care of specific functions.

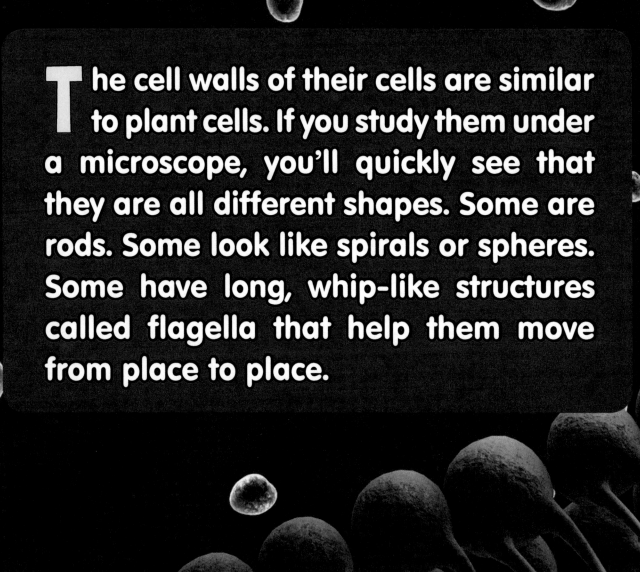

The cell walls of their cells are similar to plant cells. If you study them under a microscope, you'll quickly see that they are all different shapes. Some are rods. Some look like spirals or spheres. Some have long, whip-like structures called flagella that help them move from place to place.

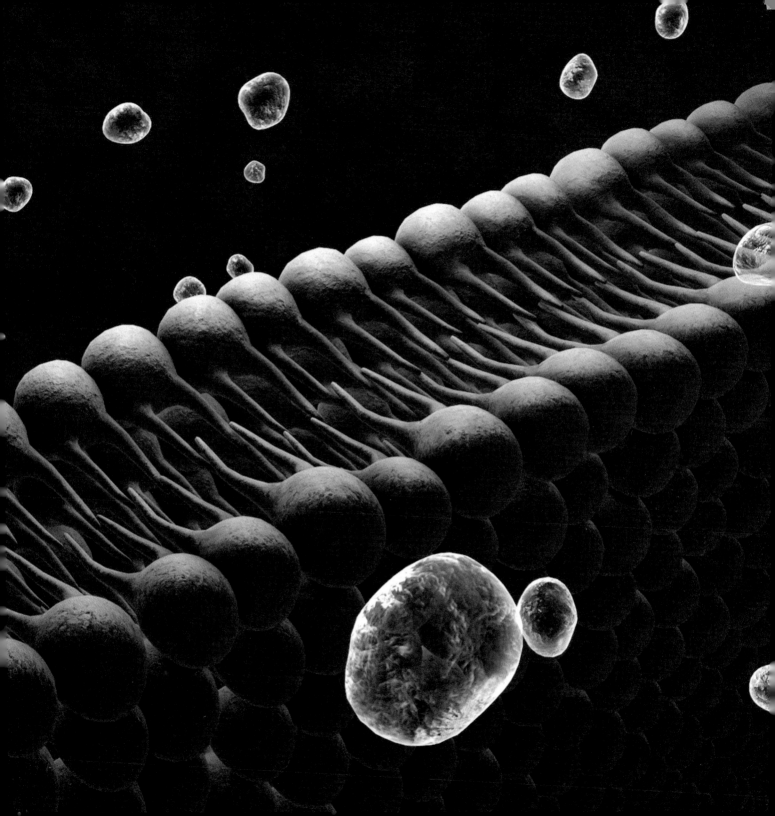

Bacteria have a bad reputation because of their role in causing a wide variety of human diseases. However, there are many species that are absolutely vital to good health. They are very important to not only human life, but all life on the planet.

For example, one species of bacteria that lives in our bodies manufactures vitamin K inside our large intestines, which is a vital factor in blood clotting. The tangy flavor of yogurt comes from bacteria and so does the sour taste of a delicious slice of sourdough bread. They're also essential for some plants, such as peas and soybeans, since they convert nitrogen to a form that the plants can use.

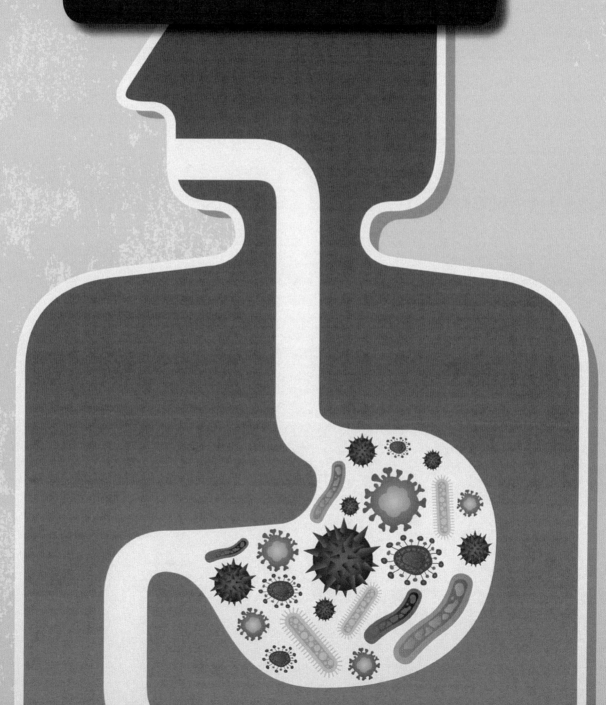

ANTONIE VAN LEEUWENHOEK

WHO DISCOVERED BACTERIA?

Antonie Leeuwenhoek was the first scientist to ever see bacteria and other single-celled organisms through a microscope. In the late 1670s, he sent detailed drawings of the bacteria and algae he had observed under the microscope to the Royal Society of London. At first, they did not believe his findings but then they confirmed his results and the science of microbiology was born.

BACTERIA ON EARTH

HOW LONG HAVE BACTERIA BEEN ON EARTH?

Scientists have determined that bacteria have been on Earth since 3.5 billion years ago. They are one of the oldest living organisms on Earth. Archaea, also called archaebacteria, are microscopic prokaryotic organisms that live in incredibly extreme conditions such as vents from volcanoes and pools that are intensely salty.

Microbiologists believe that bacteria and archaea came from a common ancestor almost four billion years ago. Although they look like bacteria, the archaea are just as different from bacteria as bacteria are different when compared to humans!

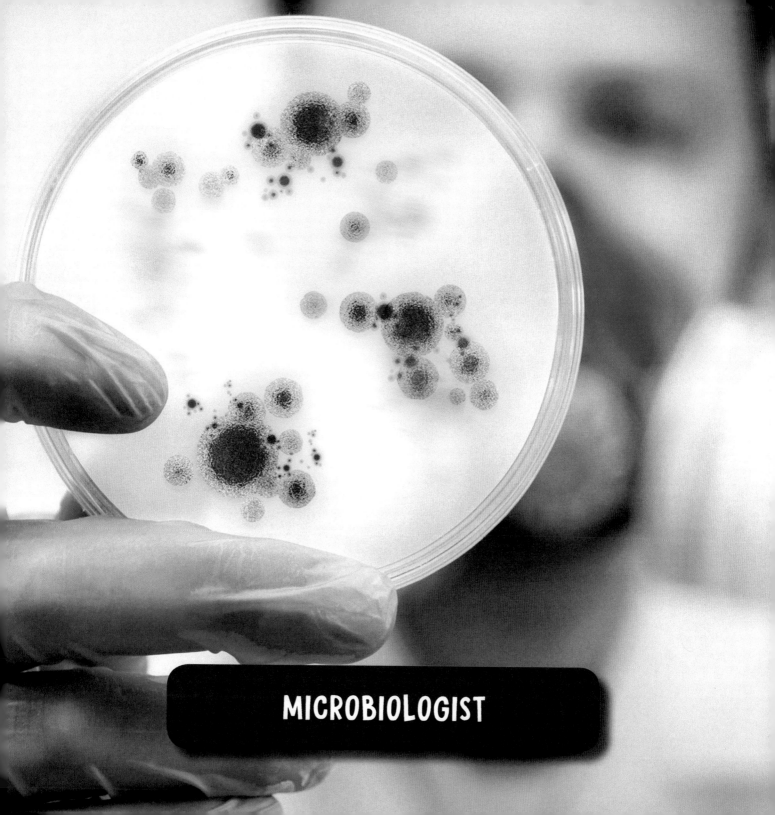

MICROBIOLOGIST

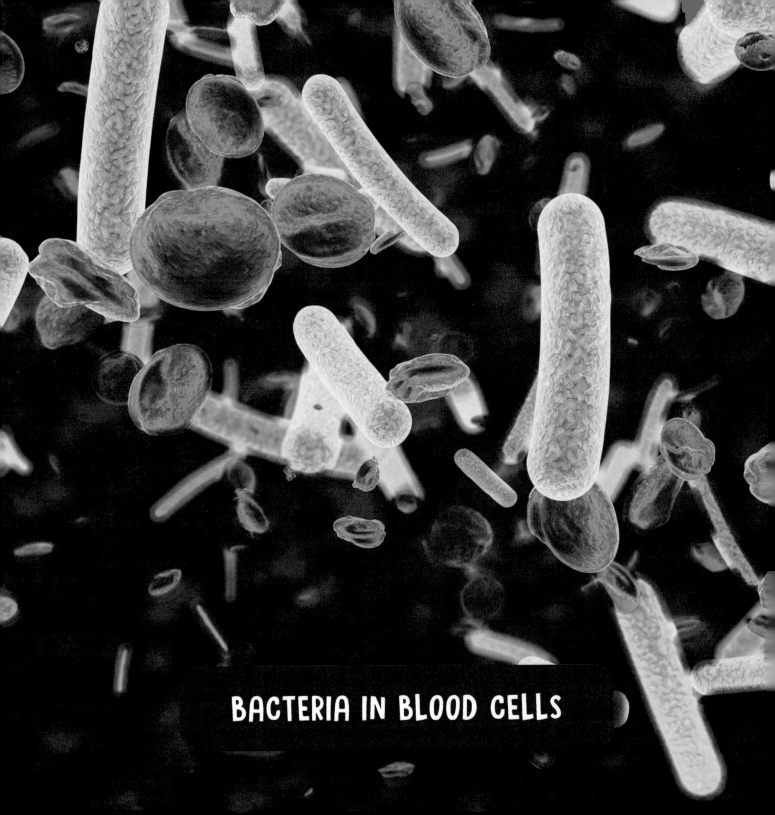

BACTERIA IN BLOOD CELLS

CATEGORIES OF BACTERIA

There are two major categories of bacteria. These categories are autotrophic and heterotrophic.

If a bacteria creates its own food through oxidation, then it's called autotrophic.

If a bacteria gets its food from plants or other microorganisms, then it's called heterotrophic.

Another way to group bacteria is by their reaction to oxygen. Aerobic bacteria must have oxygen to survive and will die without it. Anerobic are the opposite. They can't tolerate oxygen and will perish if they're exposed to it. The third type called facultative aneraobes would rather have oxygen, but they can live without it.

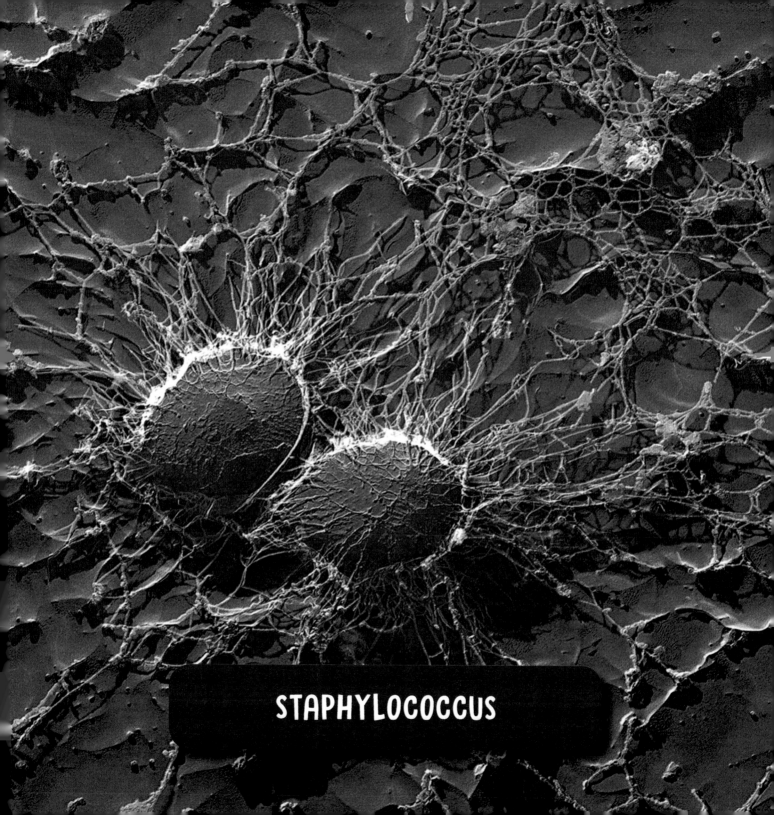

STAPHYLOCOCCUS

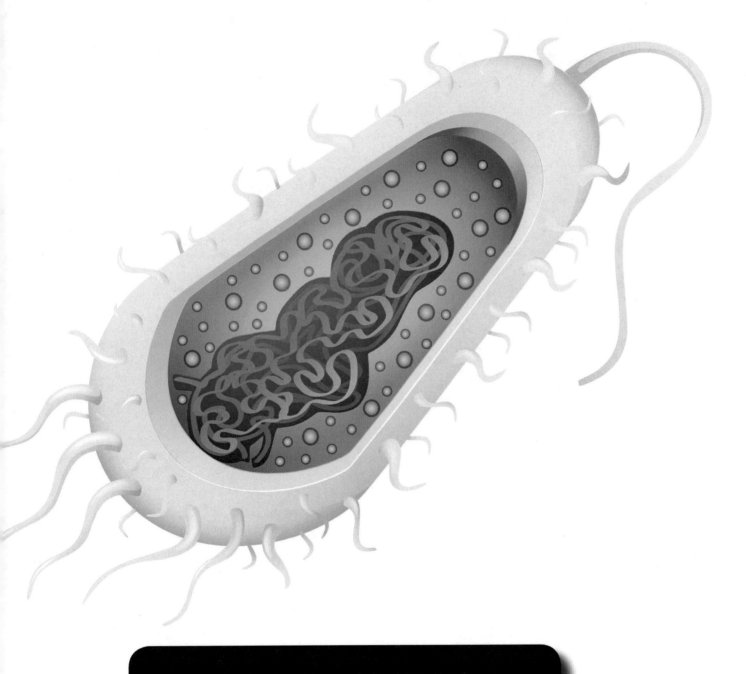

DISSECTED BACTERIA

PARTS OF A BACTERIUM

Even though the cells of bacteria don't have organelles, they still have quite a few different parts.

Capsule: Some types of bacteria have an additional protective covering. This capsule is composed of complex carbohydrates. Its role is to keep the organism from drying out and keep it from being engulfed by a larger organism. It's like a layer of slime that covers the exterior of the cell wall.

Cell Wall: The cell wall gives rigidity and strength to the cell. It protects the interior of the cell from the environment.

Cytoplasm: The cytoplasm is a gel-like material that contains the chemicals and other components needed to keep the bacterium alive.

Cytoplasmic Membrane: The cytoplasmic membrane is a barrier that allows the bacterium to regulate the flow of materials both in and out of the cell.

Plasmids: Plasmids are small circles of DNA. They play an important role in exchanging DNA between cells.

Flagella: Flagella are whip-like appendages that bacteria can use to move. They beat like propellers so the bacteria can move forward to capture nutrients or move away from something toxic. Not all bacteria have flagella.

Nucleoid: A bacterium doesn't have a nucleus but it does have a nucleoid. The nucleoid is a region of the cytoplasm where the DNA is located.

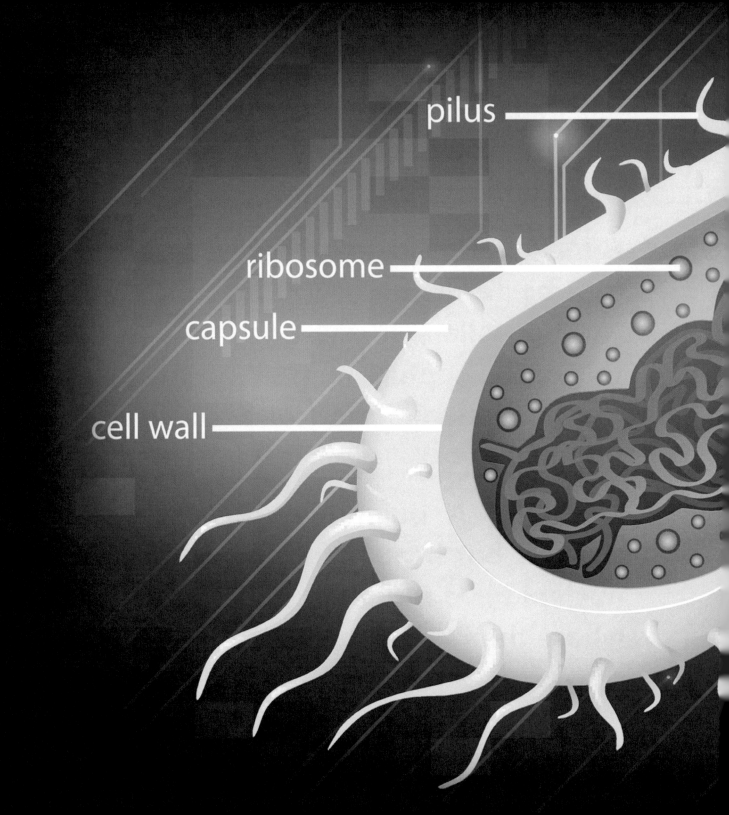

pilus

ribosome

capsule

cell wall

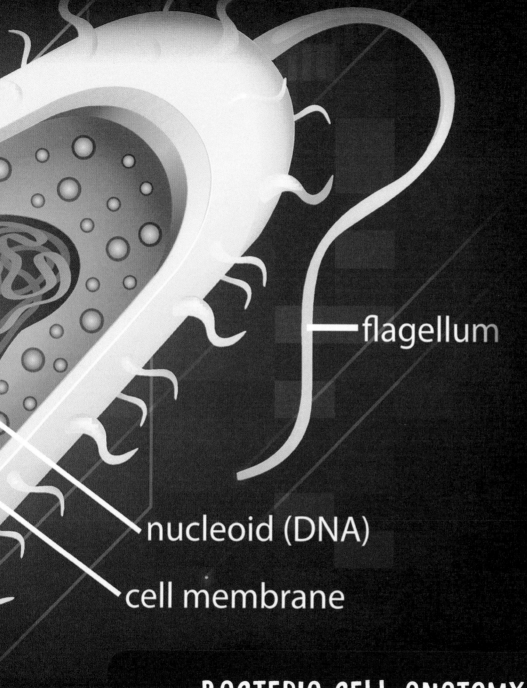

flagellum

nucleoid (DNA)

cell membrane

BACTERIA CELL ANATOMY

Food Stores: Even a tiny microscopic cell needs food. The bacterium stores its food as a globule or granule in its cytoplasm.

Pili: Many species of bacteria have pili, which are small projections that look like hairs on the outside of their cell surfaces. They assist the bacteria in attaching to surfaces such as human cells or rocks.

Ribosomes: Ribosomes are the cell structures that create protein, which is vital to repairing any damage to the cell as well as to directing its chemical processes.

Mesosomes: Mesosomes are "infoldings" of the plasma membrane and are associated with the respiration of the cell. Mesosomes are only found in prokaryotic cells and not all bacteria have them.

STRUCTURE OF BACTERIAL CELL

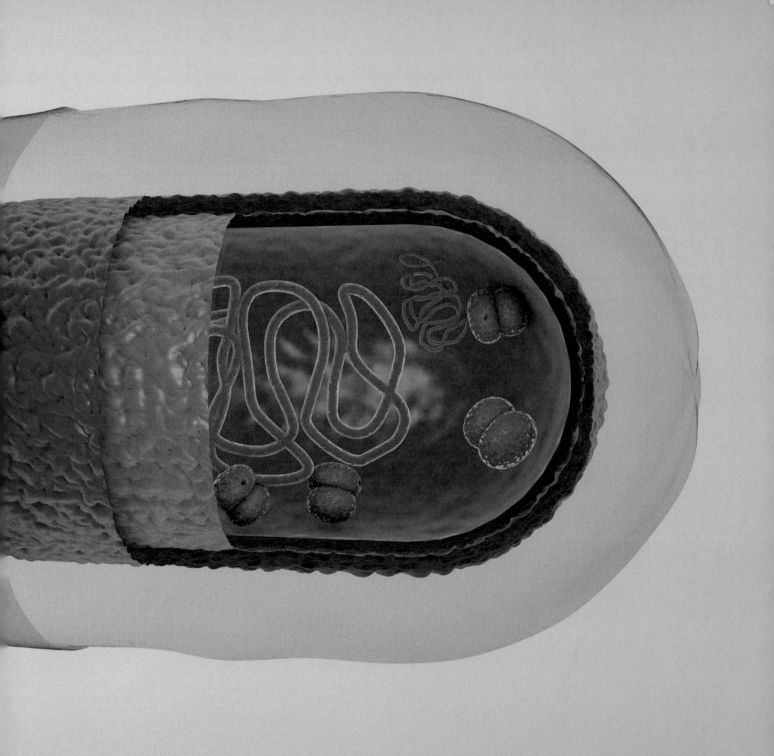

ARE BACTERIA DANGEROUS?

Most of the bacteria we come into contact with aren't dangerous, but there are some that are and they can make us very sick. The types of bacteria that make us sick are called pathogens. Diseases caused by pathogens affect both animals and plants.

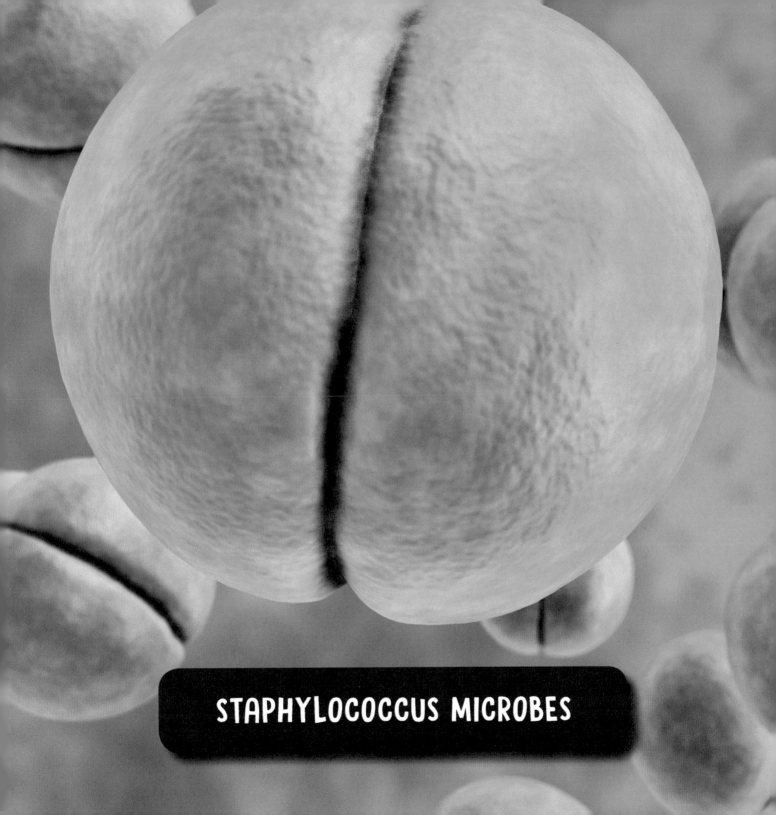

STAPHYLOCOCCUS MICROBES

In order to fight off pathogens that create disease, there are some things you can do:

- ⟴ Wash your hands well and use an anti-biotic soap.

- ⟴ Eat plenty of healthy foods like fruits and vegetables.

- ⟴ Avoid close contact with people who are coughing, sneezing, and sick.

- ⟴ Keep any wounds free from harmful bacteria by using antiseptic.

- ⟴ Take antibiotics as described by your doctor for bacterial diseases and don't overuse them.

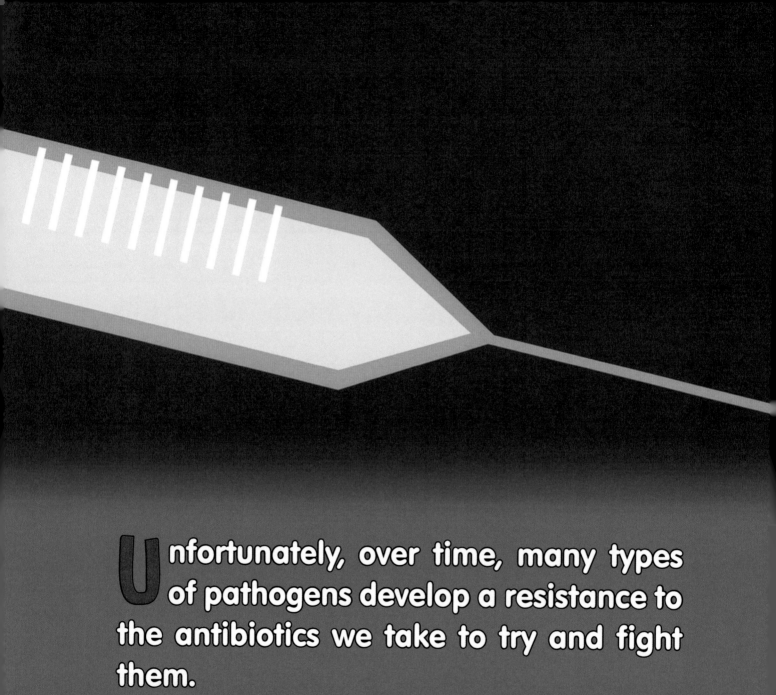

Unfortunately, over time, many types of pathogens develop a resistance to the antibiotics we take to try and fight them.

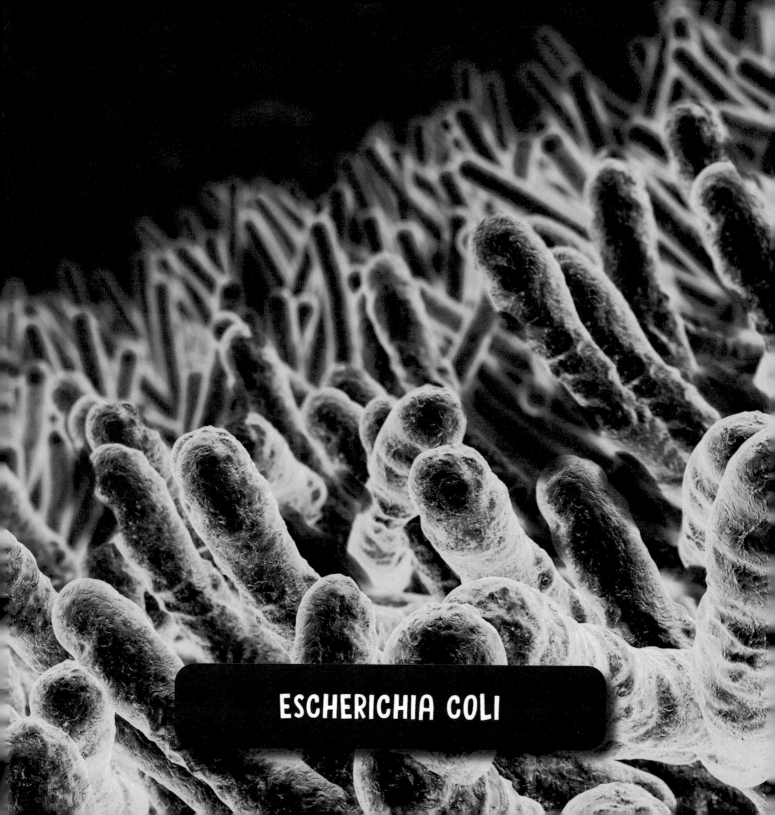

ESCHERICHIA COLI

One of these pathogens that you may have heard of is Escherichia coli called E.coli for short. Most E.coli is harmless and lives well in the human digestive tract. However, some strains of this pathogen can cause very severe food poisoning as well as infections and meningitis, a serious inflammation of the brain.

The bacteria that cause tuberculosis, called mycobacterium tuberculosis, have also become resistant to antibiotics over the last twenty years. Tuberculosis has caused many deaths throughout history and has been found in the remains of bodies 9,000 years old. Documents from ancient Egypt discuss the dangers of the disease and Nefertiti and her husband, the Pharaoh Akhenaten both died from it around 1300 BC.

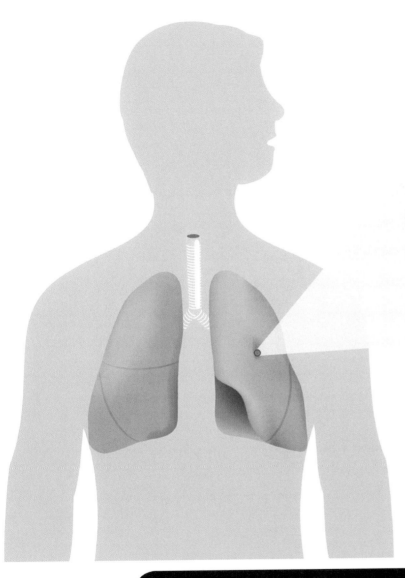

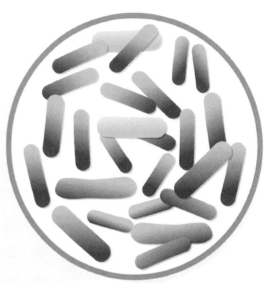

Mycobacterium tuberculosis

TUBERCULOSIS

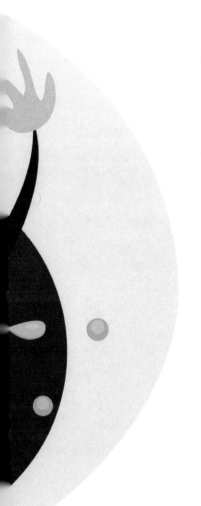

Doctors and scientists are looking for new ways to fight bacteria that are resistant to antibiotics.

BACTERIA IN THE SOIL

Bacteria and another closely related group called Archaea are the smallest organisms that live in Earth's soil other than viruses. There are more bacteria in the soil than any other type of microorganism.

BACTERIA IN THE SOIL

DECOMPOSITION

Bacteria are crucial to the process of decomposition on Earth. They break down organic dead material from both plants and animals and return it in a form that makes the soil rich and fertile. There are more heterotrophic bacteria in the soil than autotrophic, but only the autotrophic bacteria play this vital role in decomposition.

Scientists estimate that there may be as many as 40 million individual bacteria cells in just one gram of soil!

BACTERIA IN OUR FOOD

There is a lot of bacteria in our food and in our water. That's why it's important to cook food properly. For example, E. coli can live in ground meat, but if the meat is cooked to the appropriate temperature it perishes and can't hurt us when we eat the hamburger made out of it. Our water is tested for pathogens that can harm us.

BACTERIA IN THE FOOD

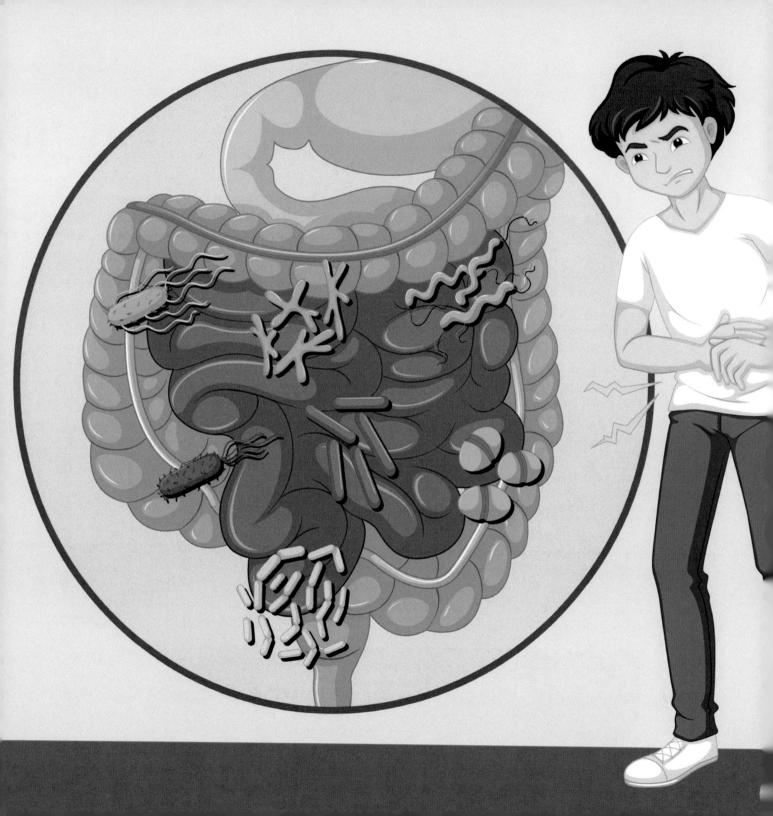

BACTERIA IN OUR BODIES

When we leave our mother's womb, we don't have a single microbe. As we start to travel through the birth canal, whole colonies of bacteria enter our bodies. By the time we can crawl, we have come into contact with as many as a hundred trillion microorganisms. They live in our throats, on our skin and in our intestines.

In fact, over ten thousand species of bacteria live in our bodies. If you put them all together, they would weigh as much as our brains. Scientists have coined a term for the bacteria that live on us and in us. They call it our "microbiome." Most of these bacteria are beneficial to us. Scientists are still learning how our bodies interact with bacteria.

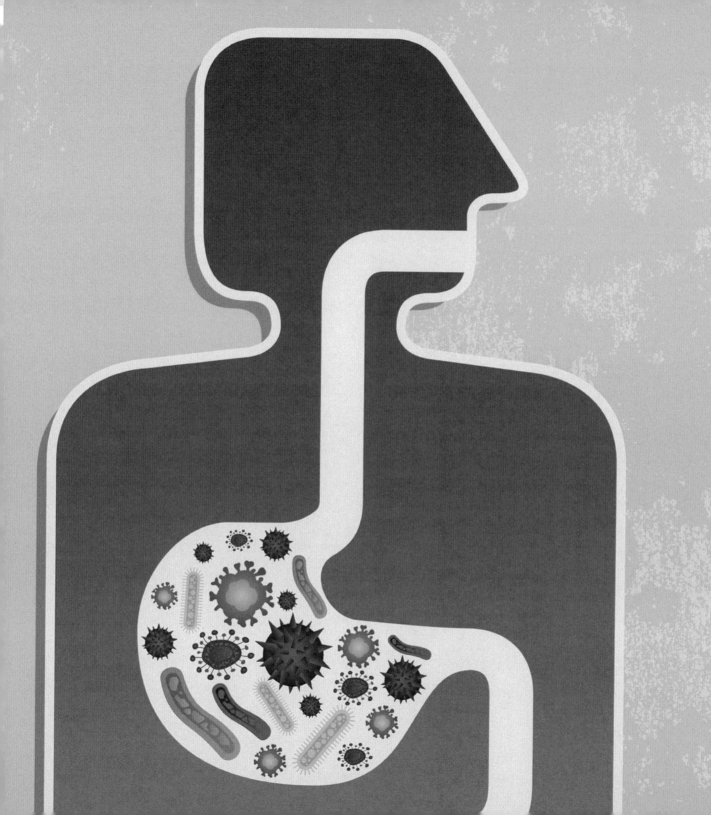

Awesome! Now you know more about bacteria and why most of them aren't dangerous. You can find more Biology Books from Baby Professor by searching the website of your favorite book retailer.

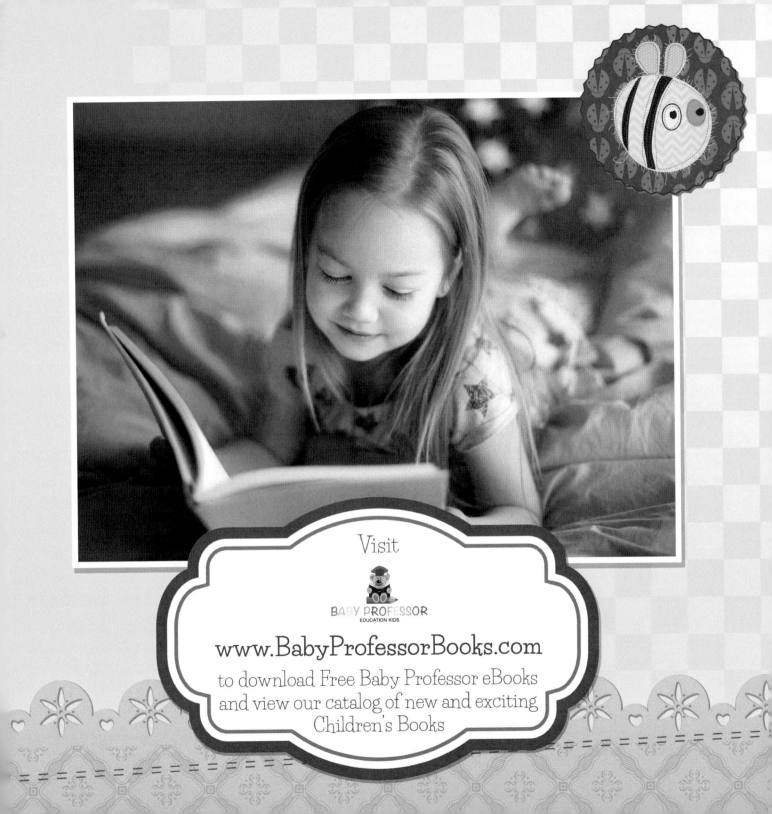

Visit

BABY PROFESSOR
EDUCATION KIDS

www.BabyProfessorBooks.com

to download Free Baby Professor eBooks
and view our catalog of new and exciting
Children's Books

Made in the USA
San Bernardino, CA
07 March 2020

65411516R00038